U.S. NAVY
Alphabet Book

UNITED STATES NAVY

SAMMIE GARNETT · JERRY PALLOTTA · ROB BOLSTER

Charlesbridge

Freedom is not free.
Thank you to the men and women of the United States Navy,
who stand ready at a moment's notice to protect our freedom.

To my husband Bill, my best friend, my all.
—S. G.

To our friend Rudy, the ultimate "bullfrog."
—J. P.

My sincere thanks to Jim "Hubbs" Hubbard and Bob "Doc" Clark.
—R. B.

Text copyright © 2004 by Sammie Garnett and Jerry Pallotta
Illustrations copyright © 2004 by Rob Bolster
All rights reserved, including the right of reproduction in
whole or in part in any form. Charlesbridge and colophon
are registered trademarks of Charlesbridge Publishing, Inc.

Published by Charlesbridge
85 Main Street
Watertown, MA 02472
(617) 926-0329
www.charlesbridge.com

Library of Congress Cataloging-in-Publication Data
Garnett, Sammie.
    U.S. Navy alphabet book / Sammie Garnett and Jerry Pallotta ;
illustrated by Rob Bolster.
        p. cm.
    Summary: An alphabet book describing the personnel, ships,
equipment, weapons, and history of the United States Navy.
    ISBN 978-1-57091-586-4 (reinforced for library use)
    ISBN 978-1-57091-587-1 (softcover)
1. United States. Navy—Juvenile literature. 2. Alphabet
books—Juvenile literature. [1. United States. Navy. 2. Alphabet.]
I. Pallotta, Jerry. II. Bolster, Rob, ill. III. Title.
VA58.4.G37 2004
359'.00973—dc22

Printed by Sung In Printing in Gunpo-Si, Kyonggi-Do, Korea
(hc) 10 9 8 7 6 5 4 3 2
(sc) 10 9 8 7 6

This book was read for accuracy by the U.S. Navy.

The authors would like to thank Jorge Acruz; Scott Allen;
Dedric D. Baker; Bob Barth; Rhea Lynn, Carter, and Laney Butt;
Bay County Reading Association; Denise Becker; Rudy Boesch;
Bruce Borgquist; Bill Bruhmuller; Bob Clark; Marilyn Daniels;
Eric Eggen; John T. Fleming; Matt Galan; Bill Garnett; Randall
Goodman; Clay Grady; Tom Hawkins; Judy Howard; Jim Hubbard;
Tom Jones; Jeffrey G. Katz; Jack Lynch; Jeanette Lynch; Diane
McKee; Tim McTrusty; John Monn; Vaughn D. Murray, Jr.; Naval
Special Warfare Group Four; Bob Nissley; Norm Olson; Mark
Olson; Eric Olson; Danny Parsons; Douglas M. Pearlman; Donna
Randazzo; Jean Remely; Bob Rieve; Tina Rockwood; Taral Snead;
Bud Thrift; the U.S. Navy; *USS Sirocco;* Curt Walters; Mike Ward;
Christy Williamson; Linda Pallotta; and Eric Pallotta.

Y page secret message: Free to Read. Read to be Free.

A is for Aircraft Carrier. An aircraft carrier is the largest ship in the U.S. Navy. It is a floating city with a crew of nearly six thousand sailors. It is also an airport with a flight deck as long as three football fields. This ship is so enormous that it has its own zip code.

Bb

B is for Boat. A boat is not a ship. A ship is a huge seagoing vessel. A boat is a small craft that can be carried on board a ship. The U.S. Navy uses many types of boats—dinghies, punts, LCMs, LCACs, WBs, SOCs, RIBs, PERS, and UBs.

The military has a language of its own. They love to use acronyms. Can you guess which boat is a landing craft mechanized, landing craft air cushion, workboat, special operations craft, rigid inflatable boat, personnel boat, and utility boat?

Cc

C is for Construction Battalion. Just call these sailors "Seabees." They are the Navy's construction workers. At a moment's notice they are ready to build an airstrip, construct a bridge, clear a road, put up a building, or repair a school for children. The Seabees have a can-do attitude. They brag, "The difficult we do at once. The impossible takes a bit longer."

Dd

D is for Diving. Hard hat divers do underwater construction, salvage, and repairs. Hard hat divers get their air from the surface through hoses. Scuba divers breathe air from a tank or from rebreathers. SCUBA stands for Self-Contained Underwater Breathing Apparatus.

EOD divers are special scuba divers who are trained to find and dispose of unexploded bombs. EOD stands for Explosive Ordnance Disposal.

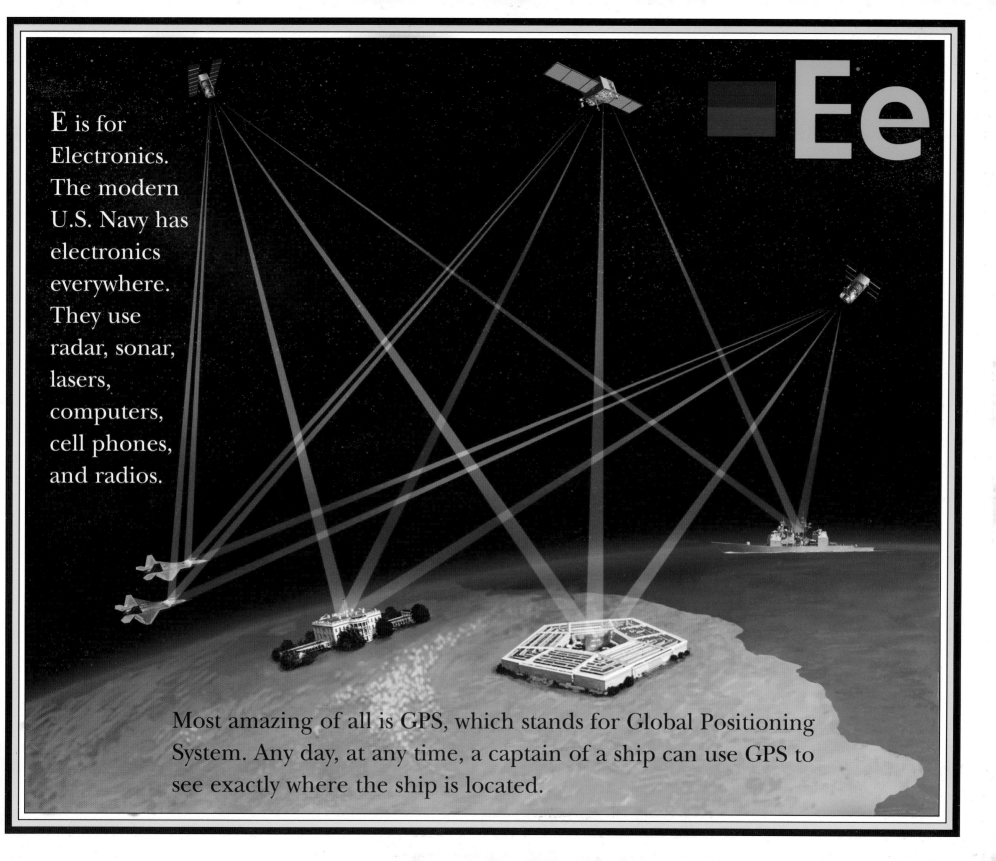

E is for Electronics. The modern U.S. Navy has electronics everywhere. They use radar, sonar, lasers, computers, cell phones, and radios.

Most amazing of all is GPS, which stands for Global Positioning System. Any day, at any time, a captain of a ship can use GPS to see exactly where the ship is located.

Ff ◆

F is for Frogman. Would you rather be called a frogman or a SEAL? They are the same thing. U.S. Navy SEALs are highly trained combat divers who are sneaky and daring. SEALs use special scuba gear that makes no bubbles and no noise. These smart commandos can attack from sea, air, or land. Some SEALs are members of the elite Navy parachute team called the Leapfrogs.

G is for Ground Tackle. This is not something you do in a football game. Ground tackle refers to the anchors, anchor cables, and chains used to hold a ship to the ocean floor.

Gg

A favorite Navy song is "Anchors Aweigh." It is played at parades, football games, and special occasions. "Aweigh" means a ship's anchor has been raised.

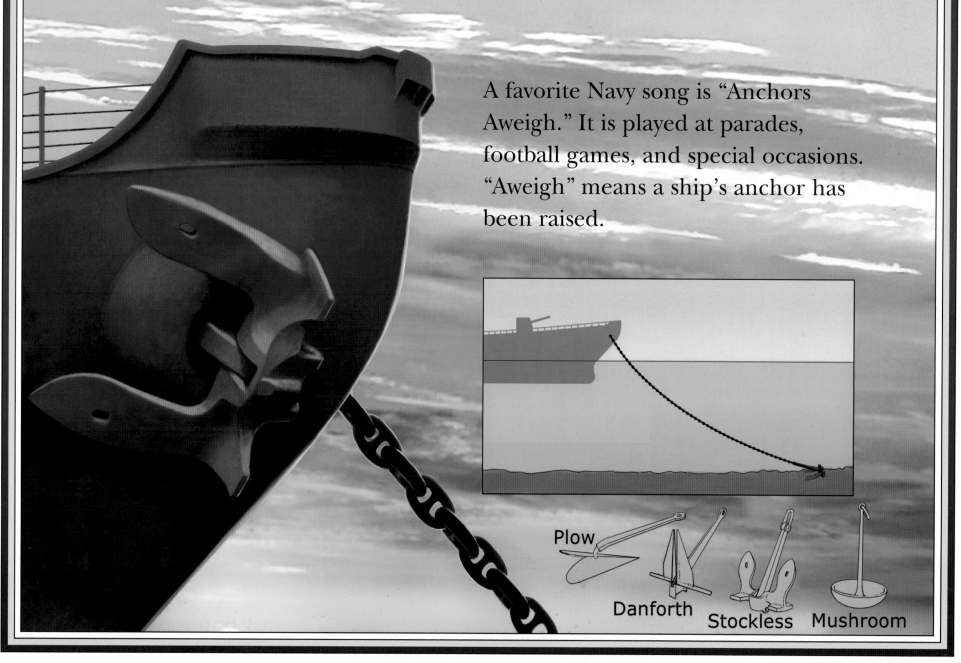

Plow

Danforth

Stockless Mushroom

Hh

H is for Homecoming. Strike up the band! Homecoming is when a ship returns from a long cruise. It is a tradition for sailors to "man the rail" while family and friends anxiously wait as the ship pulls alongside the pier. Welcome home! Let's celebrate!

I is for Ironsides. This wooden ship got the nickname "Old Ironsides" because cannon balls would bounce off her hard oak hull. In 1812 she won her greatest battle against the British frigate *Guerriere*. Her real name is the *USS Constitution*. She is the oldest commissioned warship in the Navy and is still afloat in Boston Harbor, Massachusetts.

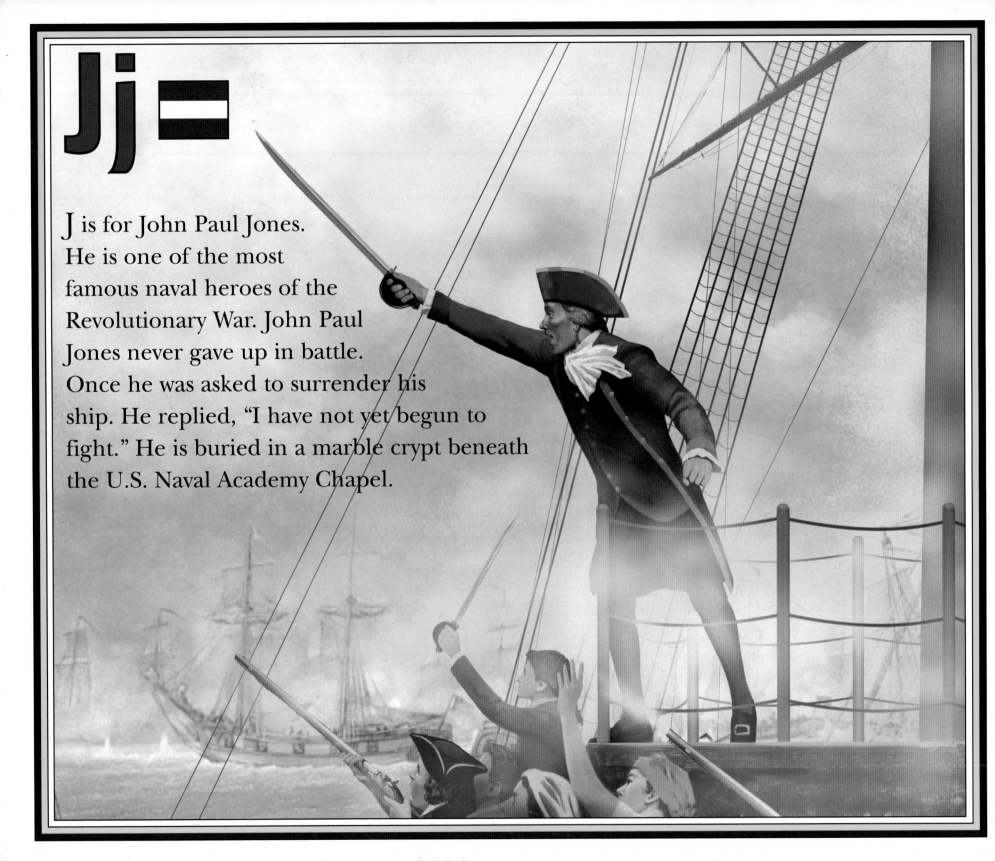

Jj ▬

J is for John Paul Jones.
He is one of the most
famous naval heroes of the
Revolutionary War. John Paul
Jones never gave up in battle.
Once he was asked to surrender his
ship. He replied, "I have not yet begun to
fight." He is buried in a marble crypt beneath
the U.S. Naval Academy Chapel.

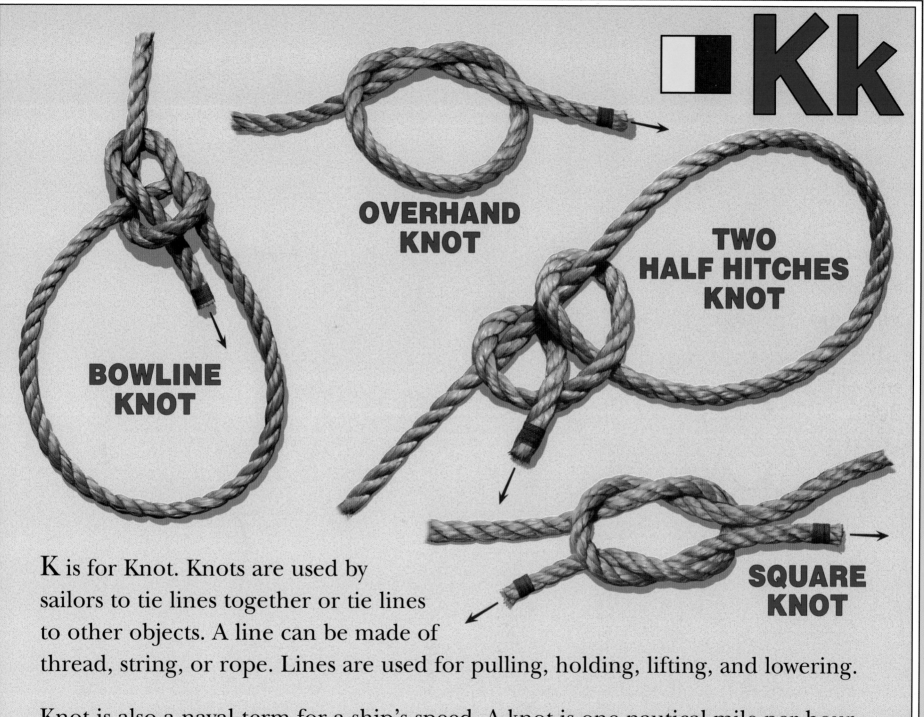

Kk

OVERHAND KNOT

BOWLINE KNOT

TWO HALF HITCHES KNOT

SQUARE KNOT

K is for Knot. Knots are used by sailors to tie lines together or tie lines to other objects. A line can be made of thread, string, or rope. Lines are used for pulling, holding, lifting, and lowering.

Knot is also a naval term for a ship's speed. A knot is one nautical mile per hour. When a ship travels at 20 nautical miles per hour, its speed is said to be 20 knots.

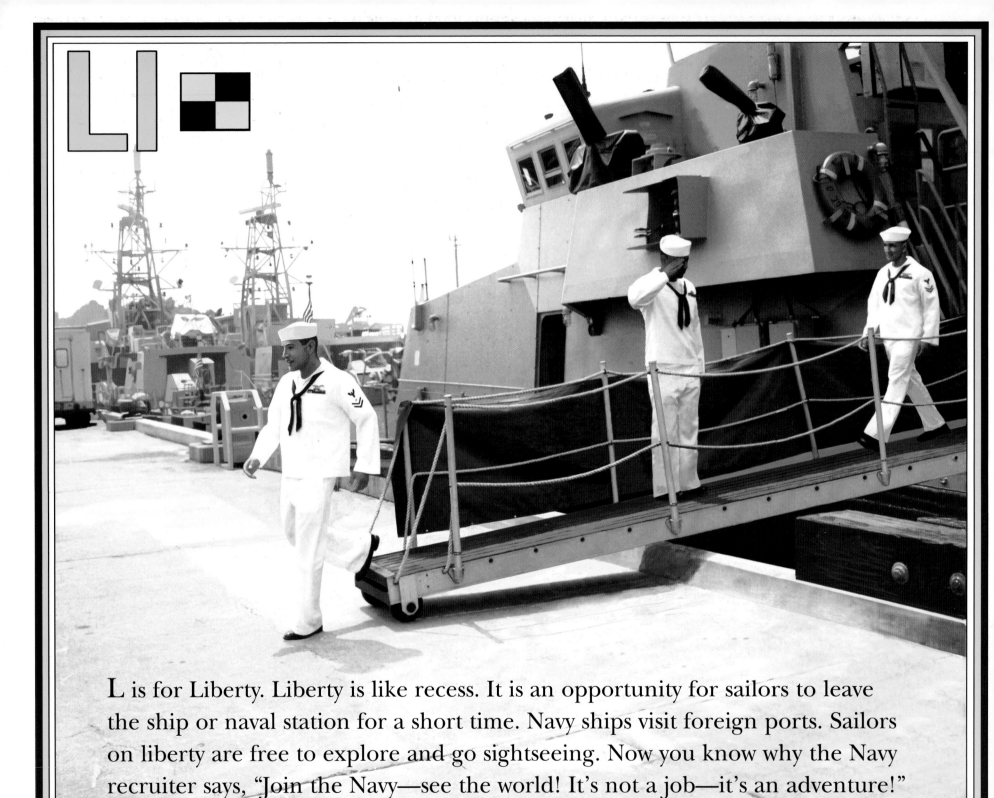

L is for Liberty. Liberty is like recess. It is an opportunity for sailors to leave the ship or naval station for a short time. Navy ships visit foreign ports. Sailors on liberty are free to explore and go sightseeing. Now you know why the Navy recruiter says, "Join the Navy—see the world! It's not a job—it's an adventure!"

M is for Medical Corps. The Navy's medical corps has highly trained doctors, dentists, nurses, technicians, and hospital corpsmen. It even has two floating hospitals. The *USNS Comfort* and the *USNS Mercy* are fully equipped hospitals each with beds for one thousand patients.

N is for Naval Academy. The United States Naval Academy was established in Annapolis, Maryland, on August 10, 1845. It is the Navy's college. The students are called midshipmen. Young men and women train to become top-notch officers while earning their college degree. It is traditional for officers to toss their hats at graduation.

Oo

O is for Officer of the Deck. The OOD is the captain's representative. The captain is the ship's CO, or commanding officer. The OOD on duty oversees the operation of the ship and signs the ship's logbook.

Pp

P is for Planes. Helicopters are known as rotary-wing aircraft. Planes are called fixed-wing aircraft. The U.S. Navy flies helicopters, planes, and jets from naval air stations and from the decks of ships. What is your favorite plane?

The Blue Angels are the U.S. Navy Flight Demonstration Team. The team was founded in 1946. They are known for performance flying. Go to an air show and see the Blue Angels zoom through the air while rolling, diving, and spinning upside down.

Qq

Q is for Quarterdeck. Everyone must report to the quarterdeck when first boarding a Navy ship. The quarterdeck is not a specific place—the captain decides where it will be. Official business and ceremonies happen on the quarterdeck.

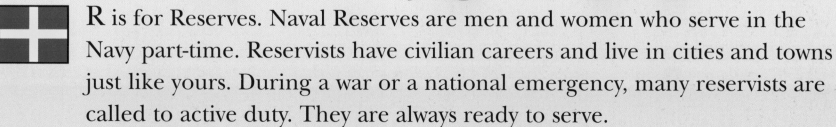

R is for Reserves. Naval Reserves are men and women who serve in the Navy part-time. Reservists have civilian careers and live in cities and towns just like yours. During a war or a national emergency, many reservists are called to active duty. They are always ready to serve.

Ss ▪

S is for Submarine. Submarines are vessels that go underwater. The first U.S. submersible ship, the *USS Holland* (SS-1), was commissioned on October 12, 1900. Do some math and figure out how long the Navy has been using subs.

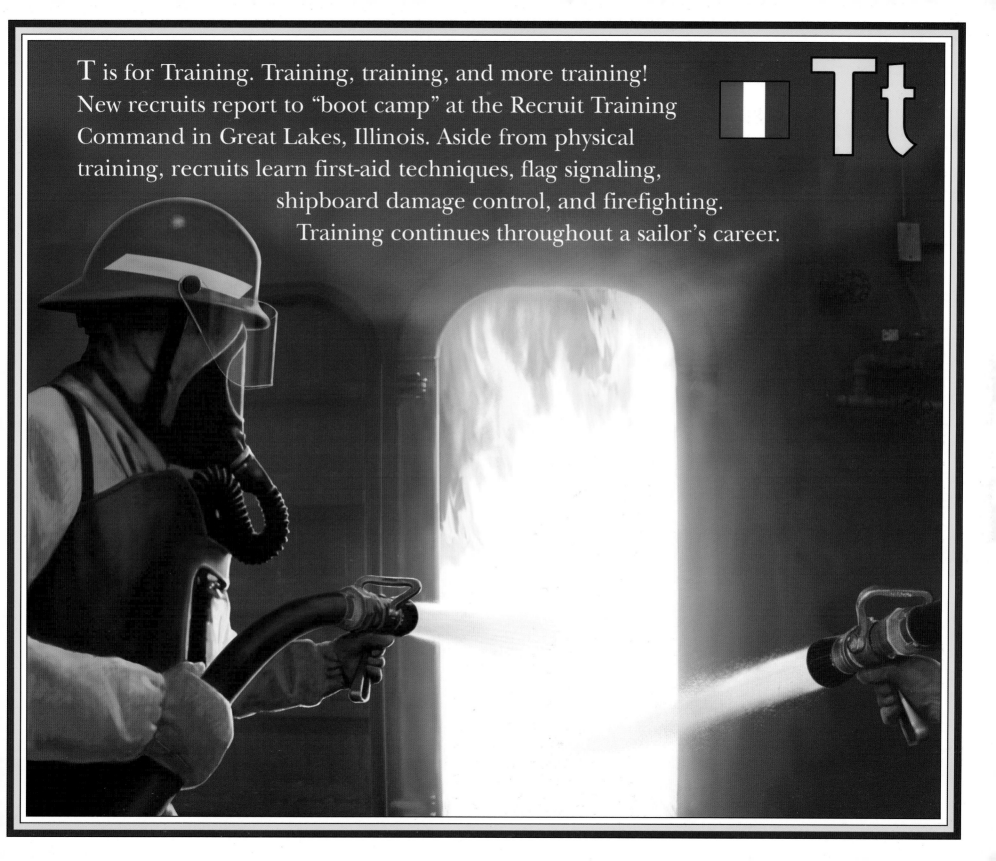

T is for Training. Training, training, and more training! New recruits report to "boot camp" at the Recruit Training Command in Great Lakes, Illinois. Aside from physical training, recruits learn first-aid techniques, flag signaling, shipboard damage control, and firefighting. Training continues throughout a sailor's career.

Uu

 U is for Uniforms. Sailors in the Navy wear uniforms. Some uniforms are made for work or combat, and some are for show or special occasions.

Uniforms change with the seasons and the weather. Usually blue uniforms are worn in cool weather and white ones in warm weather. Which uniform would you look good in?

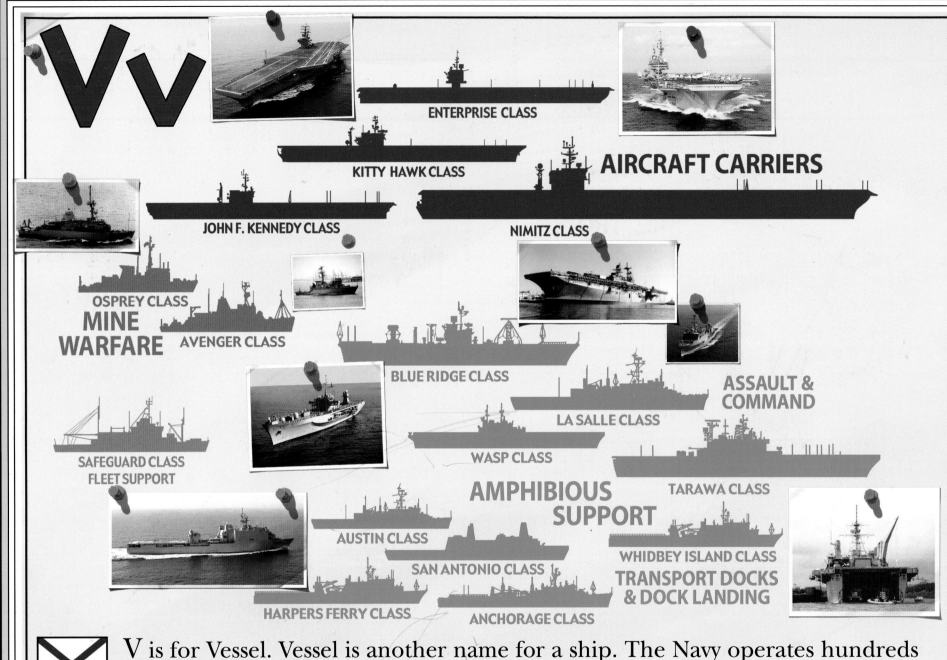

AIRCRAFT CARRIERS

ENTERPRISE CLASS

KITTY HAWK CLASS

JOHN F. KENNEDY CLASS

NIMITZ CLASS

MINE WARFARE

OSPREY CLASS

AVENGER CLASS

SAFEGUARD CLASS
FLEET SUPPORT

BLUE RIDGE CLASS

ASSAULT & COMMAND

LA SALLE CLASS

WASP CLASS

TARAWA CLASS

AMPHIBIOUS SUPPORT

AUSTIN CLASS

SAN ANTONIO CLASS

HARPERS FERRY CLASS

ANCHORAGE CLASS

WHIDBEY ISLAND CLASS

TRANSPORT DOCKS & DOCK LANDING

V is for Vessel. Vessel is another name for a ship. The Navy operates hundreds of ships. If you enlist in the Navy, would you like to serve on an aircraft carrier, a frigate, a destroyer, a submarine, a tanker, a minesweeper, or a cruiser?

The right side of a ship is called starboard, and the left side is port.

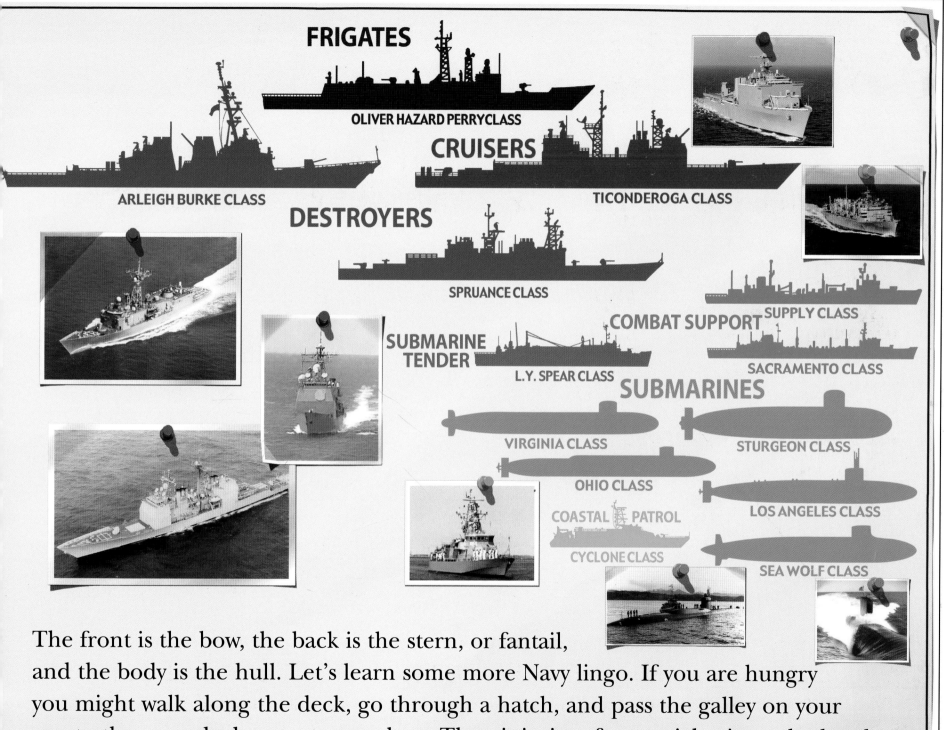

FRIGATES

OLIVER HAZARD PERRY CLASS

CRUISERS

ARLEIGH BURKE CLASS

TICONDEROGA CLASS

DESTROYERS

SPRUANCE CLASS

COMBAT SUPPORT **SUPPLY CLASS**

SUBMARINE TENDER

L.Y. SPEAR CLASS

SACRAMENTO CLASS

SUBMARINES

VIRGINIA CLASS

STURGEON CLASS

OHIO CLASS

COASTAL PATROL

LOS ANGELES CLASS

CYCLONE CLASS

SEA WOLF CLASS

The front is the bow, the back is the stern, or fantail, and the body is the hull. Let's learn some more Navy lingo. If you are hungry you might walk along the deck, go through a hatch, and pass the galley on your way to the mess deck to eat some chow. Then it is time for a quick trip to the head.

W is for Weapons. The Navy uses a variety of weapons; guns, rockets, missiles, torpedoes, mines, depth charges, and bombs. These weapons help the Navy defend the United States of America and our freedom.

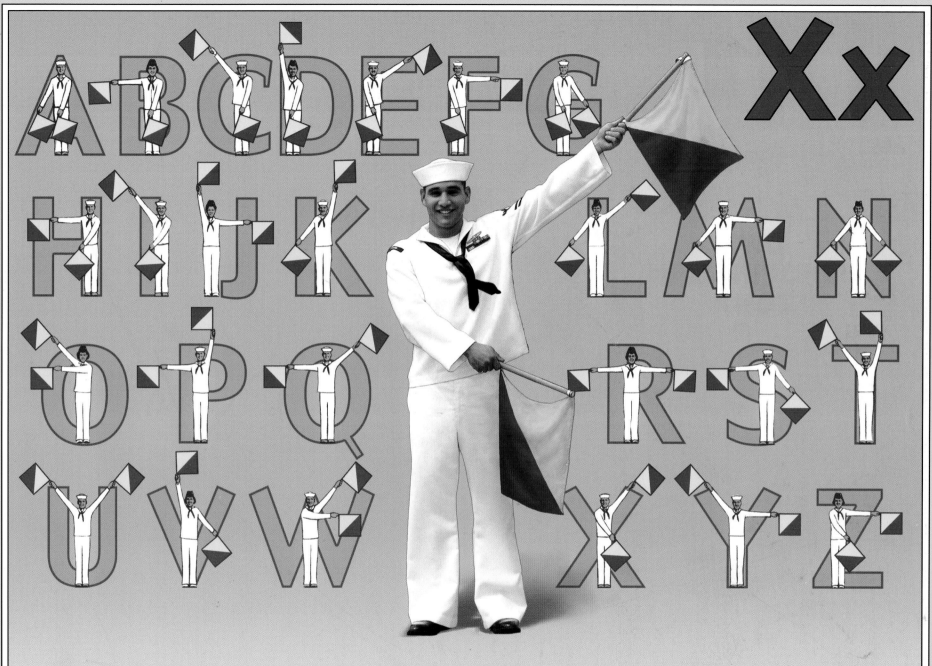

 X is for the letter X. The Navy uses semaphore for silent communication between ships. Semaphore is an alphabet signaling system. A sailor holds a pair of flags in a particular position to spell words and send messages.

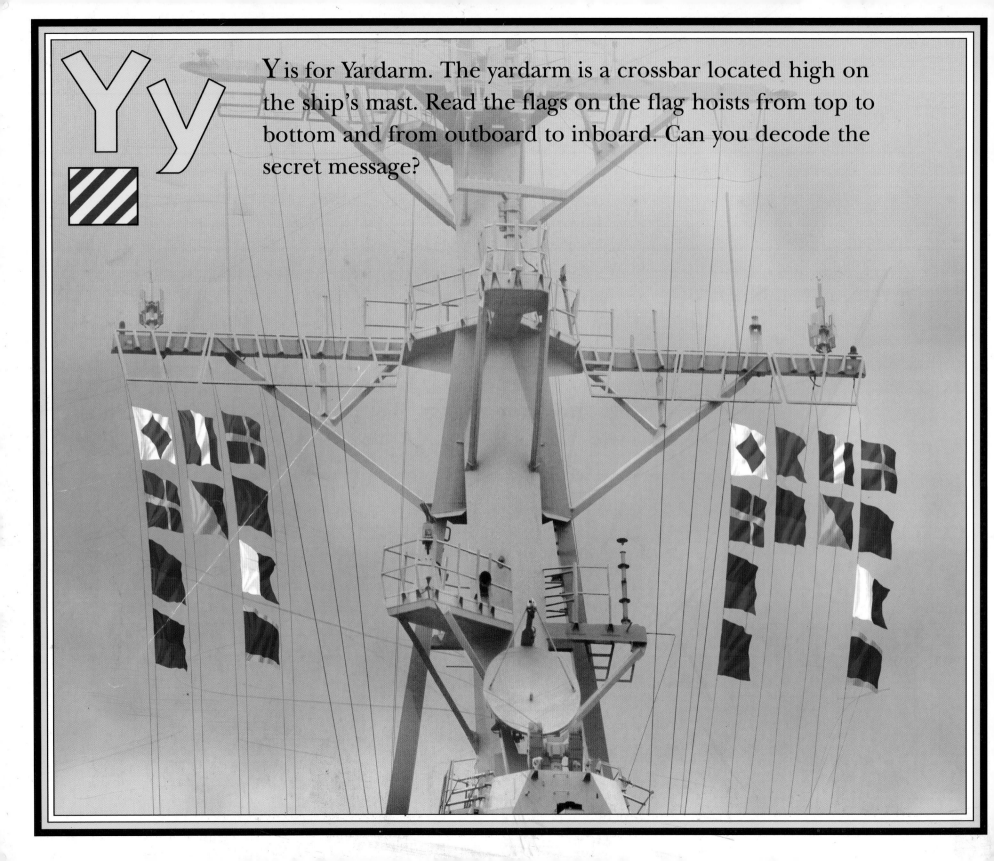

Y is for Yardarm. The yardarm is a crossbar located high on the ship's mast. Read the flags on the flag hoists from top to bottom and from outboard to inboard. Can you decode the secret message?

A............ALPHA	J............JULIET	S............SIERRA
B............BRAVO	K............KILO	T............TANGO
C............CHARLIE	L............LIMA	U............UNIFORM
D............DELTA	M............MIKE	V............VICTOR
E............ECHO	N............NOVEMBER	W............WHISKEY
F............FOXTROT	O............OSCAR	X............X-RAY
G............GOLF	P............PAPA	Y............YANKEE
H............HOTEL	Q............QUEBEC	Z............ZULU
I............INDIA	R............ROMEO	

Zz

ZULU

ROMEO....ECHO....ALPHA....DELTA

Z is for Zulu. Another alphabet! Zulu is the letter Z in the code word alphabet that the military uses when talking on a radio. Letters like B, V, T, and Z sound very similar, so the military says "bravo," "victor," "tango," and "zulu."

Honor. Courage. Commitment.